Contents

Any words appearing in the text in bold, **like this**, are explained in the glossary.

Where does your rubbish go?

You have just returned from the shops, where you bought a brand new game. You take it out of the plastic bag and toss the bag on the floor. Grabbing some scissors, you cut open a hard plastic case. Inside, you find a layer of cardboard surrounding the game. Finally, you pull it out and are ready to play.

But you are told to clean up the mess before you play your game. You grab the plastic bag, the hard plastic shell, and the cardboard. Should you run to the rubbish bin and throw them away? Or can you find something better to do with your rubbish?

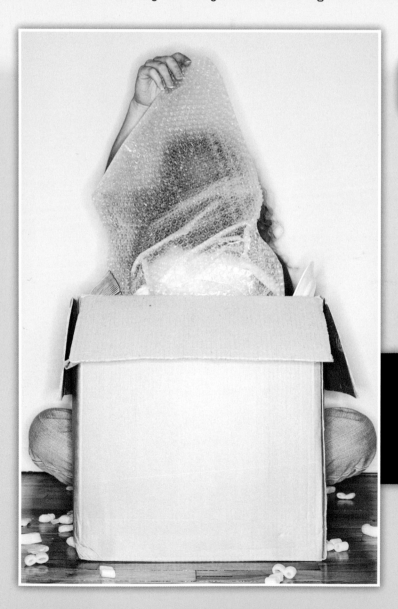

Stop and think

Before you throw something away, stop to think about what happens to rubbish. There are many things you can do to **reduce** your waste. When you make the choice to reuse and recycle materials, you help reduce waste.

What can you do with the packaging that comes wrapped around toys?

Sorting out waste

You take the bag and put it with others in a cupboard. The next time you go to the shop, you can bring the bag and **reuse** it. You cannot reuse the cardboard or the plastic, so you put them in your family's recycling bins.

Now you can enjoy your game. It took you an extra minute to clean up. But you don't mind. You have made a choice to reuse and **recycle** your rubbish. Because of your choice, there will be less waste heading to a **landfill**.

When you recycle packaging, you make less rubbish.

Making choices

Every day we are faced with choices about how to treat our rubbish. It is easy to dump what we do not want in the bin and never think about it again. But our rubbish does not disappear. Mounds and mounds of waste get carted away to landfills. When a landfill is filled with rubbish, a new one must be dug. The waste in landfills stays buried for hundreds of years.

Rubbish, rubbish, and more rubbish

People throw things away every day, including newspapers, packages, boxes, and bottles. Small things, such as leftover food, pile up in our bins. Big appliances, such as old stoves and refrigerators get thrown out, too.

The rubbish we dump is called **solid waste**. In the United Kingdom, each person throws out an average of 1.4 kilograms (3 pounds) of solid waste per day. That piles up to more than 500 kilograms (1,100 pounds) of waste per person in a year. In the United States, people throw out about 725 kilograms (1,600 pounds) of rubbish each year. In Beijing, China, the average amount of solid waste per person is about 365 kilograms (800 pounds) each year.

What happens to solid waste? In the United Kingdom, about 81 per cent of waste ends up at a landfill. The rest is recycled, made into **compost**, or burned.

Waste is buried at a landfill.

What is a landfill?

A landfill is a place for disposing of waste. A landfill could be a hole in the ground left over from a mine or quarry, or a canyon. A landfill could also be a mound where waste is piled above ground. Landfills are usually located near a road and away from houses.

Landfills are built to keep solid waste in place. A **liner** is put underneath the landfill, so waste does not leak out. The liner is made of clay or plastic. It protects the soil and water near a landfill.

Bulldozers compact rubbish before it is covered with soil.

A landfill is divided into sections. Only a few sections are filled at a time. Rubbish trucks at a landfill are checked to make sure they only dump what is allowed in the landfill. A truck is weighed and the garbage company pays for the weight of the load it dumps.

Bulldozers **compact** the rubbish. At the end of each day, the bulldozers cover the rubbish on top with soil so it has less exposure to wind and rain. As the rubbish slowly breaks down, gas forms inside the landfill. Pipes allow the gas to escape.

Not in my backyard

What happens to waste that is dumped in landfills? It sits and sits and sits! Landfills are tightly sealed, so little oxygen and water get in. **Bacteria** and other **organisms** that break things down are called **decomposers**. Most decomposers cannot live in a landfill because they need oxygen and water to survive.

Bulldozers are compacting rubbish at this landfill.

Track your rubbish

Where does your community take its rubbish? Call your city or town council and ask about your local landfill. How far away is the landfill? How large is it? Is rubbish carried by lorry, railway, or barges (a type of boat)?

Long-lasting waste

No one knows for sure how long it takes for waste to break down in a landfill, but it is a long time. Scientists at the University of Arizona dug up rubbish from a landfill to see if it had broken down. Newspapers take only about a month to decompose in soil. But in the landfill, they found 30-year-old newspapers that they could still read. The scientists dug up grass clippings, a T-bone steak, and hot dogs that looked the same as when they were thrown out. Paper took up more space in the landfill than anything else. If all the newspapers had been recycled, the landfill would not have filled up as quickly.

As people dump more and more waste, landfills become full. Many cities face the problem of what to do with their rubbish. No one wants a new landfill in his or her neighbourhood. They think a landfill will bring rats and other pests. They do not want noise and dust from rubbish trucks rumbling past. They worry about bad smells and **polluted** water from a landfill.

Rubbish trucks travel a long way to take waste to landfills.

When landfills fill up, rubbish must be transported further away. Councils spend more money and use more fuel to get rid of their waste.

Will it rot?

For this activity you will need:

* Four flowerpots of the same size
* Garden soil
* Masking tape
* A pencil
* Newspaper
* A plastic bag
* Foam pellets or other type of foam
* Vegetable scraps or leaves

1 Using masking tape, label each flowerpot as follows: Paper, Plastic, Foam, Vegetables.

2 Fill the four flowerpots one-third full with soil. Use soil from a garden if possible. The flowerpots will represent landfills.

3 Find a small amount (about the size that can fit in the palm of your hand) of each of these kinds of rubbish: newspaper, plastic bag, foam (for example, packaging pellets), and vegetable scraps or leaves.

4 Cut or tear each sample into small pieces.

5 Scatter the pieces over the soil. Put paper in the pot that is labelled 'Paper'; plastic in the pot labelled 'Plastic', foam into the 'Foam' pot; and vegetable scraps in the pot labelled 'Vegetables'.

6 Cover each pot with soil until it is almost full.

7 Water the soil until it is moist.

8 Place each pot on a shelf in a dark place (for example, a cupboard).

9 Once a week, add water to each pot so it is moist.

10 After four weeks, take a look inside your landfills. Spread out four sections of newspaper. Tip out the contents of each pot on to a section of paper. Compare what happened to each kind of rubbish. Do they look different? If so, how? Which have started to turn to soil? Wash your hands when you have finished.

Take a closer look

Were there fewer paper and vegetable scraps in your pots? Paper and vegetables are **biodegradable**. The decomposers living in soil can break them down in a short time. Plastic is not biodegradable. It takes hundreds of years to break down.

When rubbish rots, it becomes part of the soil. The scraps that you buried will break down faster in your pots than at a landfill, though. Inside your pots, decomposers have plenty of air and water. They decompose the paper and vegetables that you buried and turn them into soil.

Talking rubbish

Steps to follow

1 Tell your family you plan to keep track of the rubbish for two days. Begin by emptying the bin and asking that no one empty it again for the next two days.

2 Collect all the rubbish that your family makes for the next two days. Do not collect garden waste, building waste, or any chemical waste.

3 Ask a parent where you can sort the rubbish and spread out plenty of newspapers. Wearing rubber gloves, sort the rubbish into these categories: glass, paper, food waste, plastic, cardboard, metal, and miscellaneous (anything that cannot be classified in the above groups).

4 Label individual bags for each category. Use a sealable bag for food waste.

5 Weigh the amount of waste in each bag. Record what you find in a notebook.

 6 Add the total weight of the rubbish that your household produced. Divide by two to calculate the average waste per day.

7 Multiply your average daily waste by seven. The result will give you an idea of the amount of waste your household produces in one week.

 8 Multiple your average weekly waste by 52. The result will give you an idea of the amount of waste your household produces in one year.

What next?

Share the results of your survey with the rest of your household. Did you find items in the bin that you could **recycle**? The people in your household could also **compost** food waste. Were there items in your bin that could be **reused**? Discuss how you can **reduce** waste with other members of your household.

In most communities, glass, paper, plastic, cardboard, and metal can be recycled.

Recycling – a way to reduce your waste

Would you throw money in the bin? When people throw out paper and glass, that is basically what they are doing. It costs money for the materials and **energy** used to make paper and glass. By recycling, you save energy, materials, and money.

Recycling tip

When buying new things, check to see if they are made of recycled materials. If you have a choice, always buy recycled products.

A truck picks up materials for recycling from roadside bins.

What is recycling?

When things are recycled, they are reused to make new products. Old paper is used to make new paper. Glass is melted down and made into new bottles and jars. Aluminium, iron, plastics, batteries, and other materials are also recycled. Food waste and garden waste is recycled by composting.

Recycling helps the **environment**. Through recycling, people reduce the amount of energy and **resources** used to make things. By using less energy, less air and water pollution is created. We send less rubbish to the **landfill**. About 75 per cent of what we throw away could be recycled. Today, only 25 per cent of those materials are actually recycled.

What would happen if four families in your neighbourhood recycled all the paper they used for one year? That would save 20 trees that otherwise would be cut to make paper. Enough energy would be saved to power your home for six months!

You can recycle

Save what you can for recycling. Separate paper, glass, plastic, and other materials so they can be taken to a recycling station. The old materials are sold to factories that make new materials.

Some communities have roadside recycling, with trucks that pick up recycled materials from outside the houses. Other communities have recycling points where you can bring materials for recycling.

Recycling where you live

What can you recycle? Call your town, city, or county council and find out what material can be recycled in your area. Is recycling picked up from your home? Is there a recycling centre nearby?

People bring materials to a recycling point at a local supermarket.

Recycle it!

How many food and drink cans are in your kitchen? About 5 billion aluminium drink cans are sold in the UK evey year. Aluminium is the most abundant metal on Earth. It is part of a **mineral** called **bauxite**.

People discovered aluminium in the 1820s. Today, aluminium is used to make cans, buildings, cars, computers, and other things. Aluminium is long lasting and easy to **recycle**. More than two-thirds of the aluminium ever produced is still in use.

Here bauxite is mined from the Earth to make aluminium.

Aluminium recycling

More than half of all aluminium cans are recycled, which means they do not go to a **landfill**. Aluminium can be recycled over and over again. The aluminium in a single can may have been used many times before. Many recycled materials must be mixed with new material when products are made. But recycled aluminium does not need to be mixed with new aluminium. New cans can be made completely out of material from old cans. This is called **closed-loop recycling**. In about 60 days, a used aluminium can can be recycled, refilled, and put back on the shelf of a supermarket.

New cans can be made from old ones when they are recycled.

Making a new can from recycled aluminium takes much less **energy** than making a can from bauxite. With the energy needed to make one new can from bauxite, 20 cans can be made from recycled aluminium. Recycling one can saves enough energy to run a television for three hours or to light a bulb for four hours. Every can that is thrown away wastes energy and **pollutes** Earth.

Paying for recycling

Many US communities pay for their kerb-side collections with money earned from selling aluminium cans.

How is a can recycled?

For this activity you will need:

* Tinned foods
* Scrap paper
* A magnet

1 Use a magnet to discover how tin cans are sorted before they are recycled. Take out a variety of cans from your kitchen.

2 Label three pieces of scrap paper: A, B, C. Put each label on the table.

3 Test each can with a magnet. Does the magnet stick to all parts of the can? If so, put the can by the scrap paper labelled A. Does the magnet stick to the sides, but not the ends of the can? Put it by the label B. Is there no attraction between the magnet and the can? Put it by the label C.

What is in each pile?

The cans by the A label are made of steel. Steel is attracted to a magnet. The bodies of the cans by the B label are made of steel, and the ends are made of aluminium. A magnet does not attract aluminium. Pile C contains cans that are made only of aluminium.

At a recycling facility, cans are sorted in the same way. Huge magnets separate aluminium from steel. Then the aluminium and steel are compressed into bricks, which are sent to separate factories to be recycled and turned into new products.

Aluminium is shredded, crushed, and burned to remove labels and decorations. When the pieces of aluminium are small scraps, they are melted in a furnace. Liquid aluminium is poured into 7.5-metre- (25-foot-) long bars. The thick bars are pressed into thin sheets that can be rolled up into coils and sent to factories that use aluminium.

Steel is recycled in a similar way. The thin layer of tin that coats a steel can is removed and sold to a tin recycler. The steel is then melted in a furnace and rolled and flattened into sheets. Recycled steel is used to make cars, beams for buildings, and new cans.

Recycled aluminium is made into cans, pie dishes, small appliances, and garden furniture.

Recycling paper

Every day you use paper. You read books printed on paper. At breakfast, you might pour cereal from boxes made of paper. At school you open a notebook and write on paper. On a family trip, you take photographs and print them on paper.

People throw away a lot of paper. For every 45 kilograms (100 pounds) of rubbish thrown away, 15.75 kilograms (35 pounds) is paper. In a typical **landfill**, newspapers take up 14 per cent of the space. Paper packaging uses 15 to 20 per cent. The easiest way to save landfill space is by throwing out less paper.

Don't throw out paper. Instead, recycle it. Recycled paper saves trees and energy.

Making paper

Paper is made from the fibres that make plants strong. Most paper is made from trees. Huge forests of spruce, pine, fir, and other trees are grown for making wood **pulp**. Pulp is the fluffy fibres that make up wood. After trees are cut and the bark is removed, wood is crushed and soaked. It is cooked until it looks like a stew. Chemicals are often added to turn the pulp smooth and white. Pulp is placed on wire **mesh**, so the water drains out. Then it is rolled into paper and dried.

Paper pulp can also be made from **recycled** paper. But today, 90 per cent of pulp used for paper comes from trees. If everyone recycled their Sunday newspapers, 500,000 trees could be saved each Sunday.

These bundles of paper are ready for recycling.

Paper cannot be recycled over and over again like aluminium. The fibres in pulp get shorter each time they are recycled. Most paper can be recycled four to six times. Usually recycled pulp is mixed with new wood pulp to make paper stronger.

It takes about 40 per cent less **energy** to make paper from recycled pulp. Recycled paper uses less water and makes less pollution. When we recycle paper, less waste ends up at landfills.

New paper from old paper

1 Schools and offices use a lot of paper. Think of ways that your class can use less paper. Can you print on both sides of a sheet of paper? Set up a bin for scrap paper that you can **reuse** before it is recycled. How else can you save paper? Challenge your classmates to **reduce** the amount of paper that you use.

2 Find out what kinds of paper you can recycle and where they should be taken. Does the paper need to be sorted by type?

3 Set up and label bins for recycling. If your recycling centre requires that paper be sorted, put out different bins for different types of paper, such as newsprint, paperboard, cardboard, and office paper. Try to keep all paper out of your classroom's rubbish bin.

What next?

People have been recycling paper for as long as they have used it. You can recycle paper at home and at school. Encourage your household to use less paper and recycle paper waste.

Recycling paper

At a recycling centre, paper is wrapped into **bales.** Then it is sold to a paper mill. There, a conveyer belt moves paper into a pulper. The pulper contains water and chemicals. Old paper is chopped into tiny pieces. Scraps from the mill's papermaking process are also chopped and added to the mix. The wet scraps are heated until they form a mush, also called pulp.

The pulp is forced through screens and then spun through a cylinder. The spinning removes glue, staples, and bits of plastic that might be mixed in. The pulp is washed to remove any ink. Then, it is beaten to make the fibres swell. Chemicals are used to remove dyes from coloured papers. The pulp is whitened with bleach.

Finally, the clean pulp is ready to make paper. It can be used alone or blended with new wood fibres. Often recycled pulp is mixed with wood pulp so that the paper will be stronger.

Recycled paper is taken to a paper mill.

23

Making paper

For this activity you will need:
* Paper from your recycling bin
* A bowl of hot water
* A blender
* Uncooked broccoli
* A piece of fine wire mesh about 12.5 cm (5 inches) square
* A saucepan that is larger than the screen
* Blotting paper
* Newspaper
* A jar or rolling pin

Warning: Ask an adult to help you with this activity.

1 Put on some old clothes. Take two pieces of writing paper from a recycling bin. Remove any plastic, tape, or staples. Tear the paper into small pieces. Soak the pieces in a bowl of hot water for half an hour.

2 Fill a blender half full with warm water. Add a handful of soaked paper. Blend until the paper disappears.

3 Add three or four small pieces of raw broccoli to the blender. Instead of using wood fibres, you are adding broccoli fibres to strengthen your paper. Blend until the broccoli is mixed in.

4 Put one section of newspaper on the table and place one piece of blotting paper on the newspaper. The mixture should be the consistency of thin porridge. Add more water if it is too thick and then mix it by hand.

5 Pour the pulp into the pan. Slide the screen into the saucepan. As you lift the screen, it should be completely covered with pulp. Spread it evenly with your fingers.

6 Let the water drain through the screen into the pan. Set the screen on the blotting paper and newspaper. Cover the screen with the second piece of blotting paper and the newspaper.

7 Using a jar or rolling pin, press out the excess water. Remove the top piece of newspaper.

8 Flip over the entire stack. Remove the newspaper, blotting paper, and screen that are now on top. You now have only pulp on top of one piece of blotting paper.

9 Let your pulp dry on the remaining piece of blotter for two hours. Gently peel the paper off and let it dry overnight. How will you use your recycled paper?

More things to recycle

Recycling plastic

For this activity you will need:

* Plastic bottles
* A recycling bin
* A marking pen

1 Call your local recycling centre to find out what types of plastic they **recycle**.

2 Plastic bottles are labelled with numbers. The numbers refer to the type of plastic.

3 Look at the plastic bottles in your kitchen to find the numbers on them. Which ones can be recycled?

4 Set up a bin for your household's plastic recycling, labelling it with the numbers that can be recycled.

5 Tell members of your household what you have learned about recycling plastic. Show them where to find the numbers on plastic bottles and which ones they can recycle.

These plastic pellets have been made from recycled plastic. They can now be used to make new products.

Plastic process

In factories plastics are made from oil and **natural gas**. Some plastics are thin and flexible. Others are thick and hard. Although it seems as if plastics are everywhere, you will find less plastic in a **landfill** than paper. About 11 per cent of waste taken to a landfill is plastic, compared to 35 per cent paper.

Plastic can be recycled. Soft drink bottles and other plastics are melted down to make plastic resin. The resin is made into carpets, the padding in ski jackets, fleece clothing, car parts, flowerpots, and new drink bottles.

Today, only about 5 per cent of all plastics are recycled. In the past, it was often less expensive to make new plastic than to recycle old plastic. Oil was inexpensive. Now the cost of oil has risen and more companies want to use recycled plastics.

Recycling glass

For this activity you will need:

* Recycling bins
* Used glass bottles and jars

1 Find out how glass is collected for recycling where you live.

2 Remove the lids from used glass bottles and jars.

3 Wash out the bottles and jars.

4 Place them in a recycling bin, sorting by colour if necessary.

5 Recycle only bottles and jars. Do not put light bulbs, dishes, windowpanes, or broken glass in your glass-recycling bin.

Solid colour

Often glass must be sorted by colour (clear, green, and brown.) The colour in bottles cannot be removed when it is recycled, so coloured glass cannot be made into clear glass.

What is glass?

People have been making glass for more than 4,500 years. Glass is made from sand, limestone, and **soda ash**. These are melted together so they flow like a liquid. Hot liquid glass can be blown to shape it or poured into moulds. Glass hardens when it cools.

New glass can also be made from recycled glass. Instead of melting sand, limestone, and soda ash, crushed glass is melted. The crushed glass, called cullet, melts at a lower temperature than raw materials. Because of this, it takes 40 per cent less **energy** to make glass from recycled glass than to make new glass.

Recycled glass is made into new jars and bottles. It is also used to make insulation for buildings. Glass can be recycled over and over again.

Recycled glass is crushed before it is melted and made into new bottles.

Reuse it!

Before glass is recycled, you or someone you know could **reuse** it. You can reuse jars for a number of purposes, such as storing leftover food. In some places, if you buy a bottle, you pay a **deposit** on the bottle. To get your money back, you return the bottle to the store. The bottle is then cleaned and refilled. It takes less energy to wash and refill a bottle than to make a new bottle with recycled glass. Some countries in Europe, eleven states in the United States, and many Canadian provinces have deposit laws.

Batteries, mobile phones, and computers

Before you buy something new, consider how long you will use it. Will you still want to play the latest electronic game next year? Or will it become one more piece of waste buried in a landfill? If we **reduce** what we buy, we make less waste.

How many games and toys do you have that use batteries? In the UK 30,000 tonnes (33,000 tons) of batteries wear out every year, but less than a third are recycled.

Recycle mobile phones

There are many places to recycle mobile phones. Shops that sell phones collect them for recycling. Cities and towns have places to recycle dangerous wastes, including phones and computers. Some have special days to recycle computers.

By recycling batteries, you can keep dangerous chemicals from polluting water and soil.

Rechargeable batteries

You can reduce the number of batteries you use by buying rechargeable batteries. A rechargeable battery can be plugged into a charger and used over and over again. One rechargeable battery can save buying hundreds of single-use batteries.

Eventually rechargeable batteries wear out. What happens to them? Batteries should be recycled. If a battery contains mercury, cadmium, or lead, it is against the law to throw it in the rubbish. (Alkaline batteries do not contain these substances.) Harmful metals can leak out of old batteries. When they leak, the metals **pollute** water and soil. They should not be sent to a landfill.

Find out where batteries can be recycled in your area. Label a container for storing old batteries and ask your parents to take them to be recycled.

Reuse it

Instead of being recycled, some computers are donated to schools and other groups that need them. First, the computer is checked to make sure it works well. Parts are repaired or replaced. When a school receives a donated computer, it is ready to run.

This computer recycling centre dismantles old computers and recycles the parts.

1 Ask an adult if there is a place where you can make a **compost** pile to recycle food scraps and green waste. Choose a corner that is out of sight from your house, or away from your school.

2 Put your gardening gloves on. Ask an adult to help you make a simple frame for your compost pile using the wire mesh. It can be square-shaped or circular. The frame should be about 1 metre (3 feet) square.

3 **Bacteria** and other **decomposers** will turn your waste into compost. Decomposers need food, water, and air to thrive. In the frame, place a 15-cm (6-inch) layer of brown plant material, such as dead leaves. Brown material adds **carbon** to your compost.

4 Sprinkle the brown layer with water.

5 Next, add a 7.5-cm (3-inch) layer of green material. Weeds and grass clippings are good green plant material. Green plant material adds **nitrogen**.

6 Kitchen waste is also good green material, including scraps of fruits, vegetables, coffee grounds, and tea bags. Do not save any meat or dairy products. They will attract pests to your pile. Sprinkle the green layer with water.

7 Add a shovel full of soil to your pile. The soil contains **organisms** that break down dead plants.

8 With your shovel, mix the layers together.

9 As you collect more waste, continue adding layers of brown and green waste to your pile and watering it. Add twice as much brown waste as green waste. Every two weeks, mix your pile with a shovel. Mixing the pile adds air to the lower layers and will speed up the time it takes to compost your waste. If you do not mix your pile, you will still get compost, but it will take six months or more.

10 When your frame is full, start a new compost pile.

11 Add compost to soil whenever you plant anything. Through composting, you save landfill space and help plants grow!

Food and garden waste can be recycled in a compost pile.

Recycling for tomorrow

Every day we throw out a lot of waste. Some of the materials that we throw out can be reused. Others can be recycled into new products. When we look closely at what we throw out, we can discover new uses for our waste.

That is just what 14-year-old Michael Montelongo did. Michael lived near a factory in the United States that processed 300,000 pairs of jeans a week. The factory was left with several million tonnes of lint. Throwing away the lint cost the company a lot of money. The lint also took up a lot of landfill space.

Michael Montelongo discovered that lint from a jeans factory helped plants grow better.

A recycling experiment

Michael heard about the huge piles of lint. He wondered if there was some way to recycle it. He decided to experiment with using it as a fertilizer.

Michael planted several kinds of plant. He planted some with just soil and some with lint and soil. He measured how well the plants grew and compared them. He also looked at how the lint decomposed and if it changed the soil after one year.

Michael found that lint helped plants grow. Plants grown in soil mixed with lint were healthier and needed less water than those grown just with soil. Why did the lint help the plants? When Michael looked at the soil after one year, he found that the cotton in the lint had released **minerals** when it decomposed. He also found that the soil mixed with lint had made more air spaces. That meant that the soil held water longer and did not need to be watered as often.

Michael showed that using lint as a fertilizer was a good idea. He also showed how children can find new ways to recycle.

Think about the waste in your home, school, and community. What can you recycle? Can you find a new use for something people throw out?

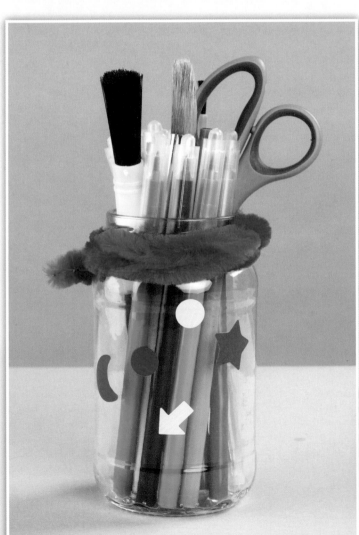

You can reuse glass jars by keeping things in them instead of throwing them away.

Making less rubbish

What's in a package?

For this activity you will need:

* Groceries from your household shopping

1 Offer to put the shopping away after a trip to the supermarket. But first, take a look at the packaging.

2 Make one pile of groceries that have no packaging. Include fresh fruits and vegetables with no extra bags.

3 Make another pile of bottles that you can return to the store, such as glass or plastic bottles with a **deposit**. When you return them, they will be **reused** or **recycled**. Skip this step if you live where there is no deposit on bottles.

4 Make a third pile that includes food packed in containers that you can clean and reuse at home. Tins and some plastic containers can be reused.

5 In the fourth pile place packages that your council recycles. Include glass and plastic bottles, cardboard boxes, and metal cans.

6 In the final pile, include non-recyclable containers and wrappers that will be put in the trash. Styrofoam and some other plastics will be here.

Making less rubbish

How can you cut down your rubbish? Look at the items with non-recyclable containers. Can they be packaged in a way that would **reduce** waste? Can you buy items that need little or no packaging? What items can you buy that have reusable packages?

Using less

Speak with others about ways to use less packaging. Discuss these tips. What other ideas do you have to reduce your rubbish?

Bring cloth bags with you when you go to the store for packing groceries.

Save any paper or plastic bags that you get at a store. Bring them back for another trip home.

Buy items in bulk. One large carton of juice makes less waste than many small juice boxes.

Reuse containers that you bring home instead of buying plastic bags for rubbish and storage.

What choices can you make when shopping to reduce the amount of packaging you throw out?

Treasures from trash

Marilyn Brackney was worried about the rubbish (trash) that she saw all around her. She knew that **landfills** were filling up and wanted to encourage people to recycle. So, she created Trashasaurus Rex.

Trashasaurus Rex is a sculpture covered with hundreds of pieces of **solid waste**. When neighbours heard about her project, they brought her old toys, watches, and other items that would have gone to a landfill. Brackney used bottle tops, sunglasses, and fly swatters to decorate the brightly coloured dinosaur.

Trashasaurus Rex's feet stand in worn-out old boots. Instead of plates on his back, he wears old, mismatched gloves. A mask with wiggly eyes makes it look as if he has eyes on the back of his head.

Trashasaurus Rex travelled around the United States to remind people to recycle. Now he lives at Rocky Mount Children's Museum in North Carolina.

Sculptures made of trash remind people to reuse and recycle.

Wrap it up

You can also use recycled materials to make your own gift bags and wrapping paper. Decorate bags from the supermarket with marker pens. Cut out colourful pictures from magazines and cover a paper bag with them. Or wrap a gift with newspaper. After you've wrapped up your gift, add a card that you've made from your recycled treasures.

Make it yourself

Make a one-of-a-kind sculpture from recycled materials. Instead of buying paper and other art supplies, use materials that might have been thrown out. Save materials in a box and see what you can create.

Here are some ideas of materials to save:

- Tubes from paper towels, toilet paper, wrapping paper
- Cereal boxes, tissue boxes, etc.
- Egg cartons
- Boxes from appliances
- Old wrapping paper
- Magazines

- Brochures
- Calendars
- Greeting cards
- Newspapers
- Add some scissors and tape, and you can create your own masterpiece!

Reuse your rubbish to make your own treasures.

Landfills for tomorrow

We can reduce the amount of rubbish that we send to landfills by reusing and recycling. But we still will have some waste, and we will still need a place to store our waste. Some landfills are being redesigned so our rubbish takes up less space. They are also being made to produce something useful.

Bioreactor landfills

Most landfills are designed to hold waste in place. In the past, that has meant that there is little air and water in the landfill. The liquid that passes through a landfill, called **leachate**, sits on the **liner** at the bottom until it is removed. Without air and water, most **decomposers** cannot live. The waste breaks down slowly.

New landfills are being designed to encourage decomposition, called **bioreactors**. In some, air is pumped into the landfill. The leachate is pumped from the bottom of the landfill into a storage tank. Then it is pumped back into the landfill, passing over the waste many times. With air and liquid pumped in, decomposers break down the waste. As old rubbish is broken down, there is more space to bury new waste.

Another type of bioreactor landfill works without air. It relies on **bacteria** that do not need air, called **anaerobic bacteria**. Leachate and other liquids pass through the landfill to help decompose wastes, creating more space to bury rubbish. As the anaerobic bacteria break down waste, they give off **methane** gas. Methane can be used as an **energy** source.

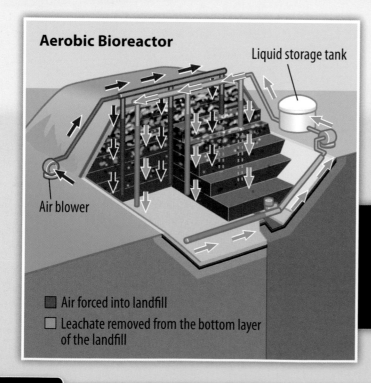

Aerobic Bioreactor

Liquid storage tank

Air blower

■ Air forced into landfill
□ Leachate removed from the bottom layer of the landfill

In a bioreactor landfill, waste breaks down more quickly.

Landfill gas

In any landfill, methane gas builds up as waste rots. Some landfills burn methane gas to get rid of it. But that **pollutes** the air and affects the climate. At some landfills, methane gas is collected and sold as fuel. It can also be burned to make steam for heat or electricity. There are more than 400 landfill sites in the United States and Canada that collect and use landfill gas.

Methane gas collected from decaying garbage can be used as fuel to make electricity.

Reduce, reuse, recycle

Every day people throw out piles of rubbish they create at home, work, and school. Groceries, games, clothes, and most goods we buy come wrapped in packaging that fills our rubbish bins. When we are done with something, we often throw it in the bin. We lose the materials used to make what we throw away. We lose the **energy** that was needed to make it. Our rubbish fills huge **landfills** and harms the **environment**.

Reduce

We can all help **reduce** the mountain of waste that we send to landfills. The first step is to think before you buy. Can you use your backpack for another year instead of buying a new one? Can you use one refillable drinking bottle instead of drinking shop-bought bottled water? Do you need to own the newest game or music player? Can you share something with a family member or friend instead of buying it?

Reuse

Instead of throwing out what you no longer need, decide how you can **reuse** it. Would someone you know want a toy that you no longer play with? If you have clothes that are too small, can you give them to someone else to wear? Can you make something new out of the materials in something old? When we reuse things, we make less waste.

Recycle

Many of the things that we throw away can be **recycled**. Huge stacks of newspapers and junk mail fill our landfills. Instead of dumping papers in the rubbish, recycle them. You can recycle glass, plastic, and aluminium, too. At home and at school, you can encourage others to recycle. As our recycling bins fill, our mountains of waste grow smaller.

All of us must play a part in solving our rubbish problem. By reducing, reusing, and recycling, we can save energy, make less pollution, and help the Earth.

You can make a difference when you start a recycling project.

Glossary

anaerobic bacteria bacteria that can live without oxygen. Anaerobic bacteria can decompose rubbish in a landfill.

bacteria tiny one-celled life-form

bale large package of material tied with string or wire. Newspaper is wrapped in bales and sent to a mill for recycling.

bauxite rock that is mined to make aluminium

biodegradable able to be broken down by living things. Garden waste and vegetable scraps are biodegradable.

bioreactor landfill that is designed so that materials can decompose

carbon chemical element that is in all living things

closed-loop recycling recycling process where new products are made completely from recycled material

compact crush and pack closely together. Bulldozers compact rubbish at a landfill.

compost mixture of decayed matter that can be used to help plants grow. When you compost food scraps, you recycle them.

decomposer organism that breaks down dead plants or animals. Bacteria, fungi, and worms are decomposers.

deposit sum of money given when bottles are purchased. When you return empty bottles to a shop, you receive your deposit back.

energy source of power. Fossil fuel, electricity, and solar power are different kinds of energy.

environment air, water, minerals, plants, and animals that surround a living thing

landfill large, outdoor area used for waste disposal. The rubbish that you throw away is taken to a landfill.

leachate liquid that drips through soil or landfills. Leachate has chemicals dissolved in it.

liner clay or plastic material at the bottom of a landfill. A liner keeps materials from leaking out.

mesh interlocking wires with evenly spaced openings. Paper pulp is lifted onto a mesh and the liquid drains out.

methane gas that can be burned and used as a fuel

mineral substance obtained from rocks by mining. Bauxite is a mineral that is mined from the Earth.

natural gas fuel that exists as a gas and can be burned for heat, cooking, and to make electricity

nitrogen chemical element that is found in the air, soil, and in plants and animals

organism living thing

pollute make unclean. People worry that landfills create polluted air and water.

pulp soft, moist mass that can be made of paper, wood, or other plant matter. Pulp is made into paper.

recycle take unwanted material and make something useful out of it

reduce use less

resource raw material used to make things

reuse use again. When we reuse materials, we make less waste.

soda ash powdery white chemical used to make glass

solid waste rubbish. By recycling, we reduce our solid waste.

Find out more

Books

A Sustainable Future, Louise Spilsbury (Raintreee, 2006)
This book discusses how to save and recycle Earth's resources.

Green Files: *Waste and Recycling,* Steve Parker (Heinemann Library, 2004)
This book explores more ways to reduce, reuse, and recycle waste.

Re-using and Recycling: Plastics, Ruth Thomson (Franklin Watts, 2005)
This book shows how materials are reused and recycled around the world.

Waste, *Recycling and Reuse*, Sally Morgan (Evans Brothers Ltd, 2005)
This book looks at the problems of producing and disposing of waste worldwide.

Websites

Where can you recycle?
www.recyclenow.com
Find out where to go and what you can recycle in your area.

The Environment Agency
www.environmentagency.net/fun
Learn lots of ways to reduce, reuse, and recycle, while having fun.

Why and how to recycle
www.recycling-guide.org.uk
Find up-to-date news and fun recycling activities here.

Reduce food waste
www.lovefoodhatewaste.com
Practical tips on how to reduce the amount of food we waste and throw away.

Organizations

The Environment Agency

www.environment-agency.gov.uk

This leading public organization works for a cleaner, healthier environment for all.

WRAP

The Old Academy
Horse Fair
Banbury, Oxfordshire
OX16 0AH

www.wrap.org.uk

An organization that helps individuals and businesses to reduce waste and recycle more.

Places to visit

The Eden Project

Bodelva
St Austell
Cornwall, PL24 2SG

www.edenproject.com

Centre for Alternative Technology

Machyblleth
Powys, Wales
SY20 9AZ

www.cat.org.uk

The Centre for Alternative Technology shows how we can work towards achieving zero waste.

Index